# the
# Warning

(Cum permisso superiorum)

## by Father Philip Bebie, C.P.

# Explanation of This Book

A great struggle between good and evil is going on. Pope Paul VI did not hesitate to call it "apocalyptic."

The ultimate result of this struggle was told to us *specifically* at Fatima: There will be a triumph of love . . . a triumph of the Immaculate Heart of Mary . . . "Russia will be converted and an era of peace will be granted to mankind."

Before that triumph we may have a terrible chastisement in which "several entire nations will be annihilated."

According to Garabandal, Medjugorje, etc., to make it possible for the world to avoid that chastisement the Queen of Peace has obtained for us THE WARNING.

Holy prophets (Saint Edmund Campion, Blessed Anna Maria Taigi) predicted this same warning at the very beginning of the historical religious catastrophies: The Reformation conflicts (Saint Edmund Campion) and the rise of Marxism (Blessed Anna Maria) which have brought our world to its present state of estrangement from God.

At the time of the publication of this book in 1986 Father Bebie (who wrote this in 1981-82) was suffering the final stages of a terminal cancer, which, to the surprise of his doctors and most of all to himself, had not yet taken his life. He had previously entrusted the manuscript to a friend to be published *when* the warning occurred. During a "goodbye" visit early in 1986 . . . shortly after he had returned from a hospital intensive care unit, it was decided that publication after the warning might be ineffective. It might be too late for people to know *the importance of what had just happened to them* . . . and to the world!

THE IMPORTANCE OF THIS WARNING CANNOT BE EXAGGERATED.

*It will be an act of God . . . an act of His Mercy. Whether the world will avoid annihilation of several entire nations* will depend on how each of us reacts to this act of His Mercy.

At a time when the world has lost its sense of sin, we will suddenly see ourselves as God sees us. We will recognize our sins.

IF WE REJECT THIS ACT OF MERCY. . .if we then persist in our sins . . . will we not deserve to see the whole world purged with fire . . . or by whatever purging Divine Justice may elect?

It is possible that many will reject the warning out of ignorance.

That is why it seemed both prudent and advisable to make this book available *in advance,* entrusting to those who receive it, the *responsibility* of communicating with newspapers, television, radio, Church leaders, government officials, in a word, to all who will be able to inform the greatest number of people just what the warning means as soon as it happens.

It may be a year away. It may happen tomorrow. There are many indications that it will come *soon.*


NOTE: Father Bebie died in 1986, when at the very time this little book (written by him in 1981) was being printed.

# Foreword

Blessed Anna Maria Taigi spoke of a great chastisement which would come to the world before which there would be *an illumination of the conscience of men* by which suddenly everyone would see themselves as God sees them. She indicated that this illumination of conscience would result in the saving of many souls because many would repent as a result of this "Warning" . . . this miracle of "self illumination".

Beatified in 1920 as a model of women and mothers, Anna Maria Taigi was not only a prophetess of our time, but one of the most extraordinary mystics in the history of the Church.

From the time she was 20 years old, until she died at the age of 63, the Beata was accompanied by a mysterious light in which she saw past, present, and future events . . . some relating to struggles among nations; some relating to individual souls.

Blessed Anna Maria gazed into that light only when she felt an interior impulse . . . a sort of direction from Our Lord and the Holy Spirit . . . to do so. And usually when she looked into the light she was asked to offer some special suffering for a special need in the Church or in an individual.

In that light Anna Maria saw a great chastisement coming upon the world in the future . . . but at the same time a *great blessing: The "Warning" which would be an illumination of the consciences of men, just as though suddenly every man was given the same kind of light that accompanied her . . . in which they would see themselves as God sees them.*

It is interesting that 300 years before Blessed Anna Maria this same revelation was given to St. Edmund Campion, who went to his death affirming this same prophecy.

One is put in mind of the prophecies of the Old Testament . . . some of which were close to the time of Our Lord, and some of which were hundreds of years before. And no one ever knew with any exactitude when those prophecies would be fulfilled.

But we now have cogent reasons to believe that this prophecy of the warning and the chastisement ... which we have heard from the lips of various good persons and canonized saints ... will take place very soon, for we recall that St. John Bosco, an authentic prophet of our time, was told by Our Lady that She would obtain a victory for Christianity before the year 2000 which would be greater even than the victory of Lepanto (which in 1571 was a turning point in the history of the world over seemingly hopeless odds).

Father Philip Bebie, a Passionist priest who became nationally celebrated for his book "Proclaim Her Name" (A.M.I. Press) was a founding member of a Passionist House of Solitude and was Administrator of the first two Charismatic Priests' conferences in Steubenville, Ohio (1975–76). He then preached Parish Missions until his sickness (1983).

The year 1985 was the jubilee (25 years) year of his priesthood. During this recent time of grace Father Philip became convinced that the foretold warning (and at the same time great miracle of grace) would find most people unprepared. He felt a need to explain the Garabandal prophecies so that when the world experienced the illumination of conscience people would better know what it meant and be prepared for the Great Miracle.

Father Philip began this book in October of 1981 and completed it January 1st, 1982. He did not intend that it should be published until after the Warning took place. But he shared the manuscript with a few friends. One of them allowed Father Philip himself to set the manuscription into print so that it would be ready for immediate printing and distribution when The Warning occurred.

Four years later, Father Philip himself was dying of an advanced state of cancer of the liver. And while constantly thinking of his imminent death, he also began to sense the possibility that he himself might still be alive to experience the Warning and the great Miracle that is to follow. It then occurred to some of his friends that since the predicted time between the Warning and the Miracle would be less than a year, it might be best to have some copies of this book printed in advance and in the hands of at least some people in different parts of the world so that it would be more readily available if and when these prophecies are actually realized.

It must be borne in mind that this book is intended to be published generally only after the Warning. For that reason it reads as though the miracle of illumination of conscience had already been experienced by the reader. Even if read before the Warning we believe it will be of deep interest and edification for all who read it.

Ask the 101 Foundation about the
*— Garabandal Miracle Flight —*

This book does not anticipate the judgment of the Church on the events of Garabandal. It is intended for publication only AFTER the final major prophecy of Garabandal—The Warning—will already have taken place.

To be ready for that event a limited number of copies is being distributed in advance. They are not for sale. However, an offering for postage (tax-deductible) would be appreciated.

Printed with permission of the ecclesiastical superior.

*Books Available in the U.S. from:*

The 101 Foundation, Inc.
P.O. Box 151
Asbury, NJ 08802-0151
Phone: 908-689 8792
Fax: 908-689 1957
www.101foundation.com
email: 101@101foundation.com

# Contents

# TODAY
## *(The Warning)*

*The Warning . . . predicted by Our Lady of Mount Carmel . . . was like the conversion of Saint Paul . . . made us aware of God . . . shows us our sins . . . was a taste of eternity . . . was a mercy from God . . . is a sign of the future . . . is a direct intervention of God . . . calls us to choose . . . calls us to prepare for The Miracle . . . is inseparable from The Miracle.*

# YESTERDAY
## *(Mary's Past Warnings)*

*Paris 1830 . . . LaSalette 1846 . . . Lourdes 1858 . . . Fatima 1917 . . . Garabandal 1961.*

# TOMORROW
## *(After The Warning)*

*One person knows the date . . . one person has seen it . . . millions will see it . . . will be a revelation . . . will be Eucharistic . . . will be ecclesial . . . will be Marian . . . will convert the world . . . will be sacramental . . . will be a warning . . . will be for the glory of God.*

*Will take place after The Miracle . . . will be directly from God . . . will purify the earth . . . will be the last punishment . . . will not be the end of the world . . . will not be a war . . . no one will escape it.*

*A reminder of the message . . . it calls us to holiness . . . it will point us toward heaven . . . it will guard the era of peace.*

# THE NEXT DAY
## *(The Triumph)*

*"My Immaculate Heart will triumph" . . . it is victory over evil in hearts . . . it has already begun . . . it will glorify Mary . . . it will be a conversion event.*

*It has been delayed . . . prayer hastens it . . . penance and reparation hasten it . . . amendment of life will hasten it . . . Consecration will hasten it.*

*Consecration is a form of devotion . . . consecration is a simple matter . . . Consecration opens us to God's power.*

*"There will be peace" . . . The Era of Peace awaits the Triumph. . . The Era of Peace can come soon.*

# THE NEW TIMES
## *(The Evangelization of the World)*

*The whole world will be converted . . . this has happened before . . . a third world-evangelization will begin soon . . . the Church is being prepared . . . the whole world will be evangelized . . . The Warning prepared the Church for evangelization . . . the Churches will be reunited . . . God will unite us . . . Russia will be converted . . . the new Church will be humble . . . the reunited Church will be the Sign of evangelization . . . conversion takes time . . . what will the new Church of the Era of Peace be like?*

# Introduction

A short time ago, abruptly, all on earth felt the intervening of God. To each one of us He unveiled the innermost secrets of our heart. His inexorable light seared our consciences and showed us to ourselves as in a flawless mirror. The truth was vivid in our minds. We saw the awful blight of our sinfulness, the excruciating pain of it, and knew in an instant what our eternity would be because of it. The Lord's mercy scoured away all pretension. By His merciful intrusion, we knew ourselves --- oh, how we knew ourselves, in His light. We felt The Warning.

Over twenty years ago it had been predicted by the Mother of God, who communicated her message to us through four young girls from the mountain village of Garabandal, Spain, remote and rude, rocky and high, among the clouds. The message was plain as well, and not really new in content, for she had been repeating it generation upon generation as she visited one place after another for what is now a span of one hundred and fifty years. Yet at this moment she had spoken it with special urgency. Time was running out. These would be the "last warnings" the world would receive. People would have to change their lives and stop offending God, or else they would suffer the most terrible consequences.

The four children who saw her were informed of great events that would overwhelm the world. These occurrences were to happen, by God's great mercy, so that the whole world would be converted. They would bring about the conversion of humanity. But unless we heard the message and changed soon, this would happen only after great suffering.

She told them of "The Warning", a "correction of the conscience of the world", which all would experience as a kind of disaster in their lives, but none would die of it, except perhaps from the shock of it. She also spoke to them of a "Great Miracle" to be worked by the Lord at Garabandal so that we all might come to believe, but she would not permit the disclosure of the exact time this would happen (although one of the girls knows the date and must announce it eight days before it happens). Lastly she revealed to them "The Punishment", which would descend upon us "directly from God", if people did not repent in time to avert it.

The Punishment *must be avoided. Because the Lord wants to protect us from it, He gives us The Warning* and *The Miracle.* They are meant to help us respond to the message of Mary so that we can avoid The Punishment entirely. We must understand what to do to be saved, and then we must do it. Our fate hangs in the balance. There will be peace; Our Lady of Fatima has promised that it will inevitably arrive. What we do between now and that *"Era of Peace"* will determine whether or not The Punishment will first have to be undergone.

But for now, we know that *The Warning* has pierced our hearts. We have known it with greater clarity than anything else has ever been known. We must heed it, and look again at the repeated messages and warnings of the Mother of God. Looking again and more deeply is the burden of this book.

We will recall and reflect upon what she said over the long years of our forebears, consider the present situation, and open up to her promises. There is danger, greater danger than humankind has ever faced before, but there is also hope. She asserted, "There will be peace." "In the end My Immaculate Heart will triumph; the Holy Father will consecrate Russia to Me. Russia will be converted, and an *Era of Peace* will be given to the world."

This book will attempt to answer many of the questions on your mind since you felt *THE WARNING*. What was *the Warning?* Is a Miracle coming too? Why has the whole world been involved in such a powerful, direct way? Is it the end of the world?

Read and be instructed. All the material presented has been around for twenty years, but we have not heard it, or been prevented from hearing it. God has broken through the darkness. Read now. It is time.

# TODAY

# Chapter One

# The Warning

The Warning was predicted by Our Lady of Mount Carmel at Garabandal, where she prophecied three great events that were to come: The Warning, The Miracle, and The Punishment. The last would occur only if the world would still refuse to repent after the first two made God's mind plain to all. We have just experienced the first; the second and third are still in the future. The Miracle will come within a year of The Warning, so that we will be prepared to receive the grace of The Miracle.

The Warning *was like the conversion of Saint Paul the Apostle*, who was penetrated by the same light we have recently endured. He was on the Damascus road, journeying to that town to persecute the newly converted Christian Jews who lived there. In a glorious vision it was revealed to him that he was assailing not only the members of the Church, but Jesus Himself, the very Lord of heaven and earth! The blinding light of the Risen Christ convicted him of sin. Paul heeded the warning Jesus had given him; he repented and became his faithful follower, and left his former life behind.

Has not the same enlightenment been accorded to us all in The Warning? The grace once granted to an individual has finally penetrated every human heart in a single, sudden burst of divine light. We have felt the same grace, the same light, that Paul did. God would have the whole world respond just as Paul did. We must now repent of the sin the Lord has shown us in ourselves by The Warning, and amend our lives, following Jesus.

The Warning *made us aware of God.* Everyone, unbeliever as well as believer, now can declare that God has touched us with His immeasurable power. He has intervened in an unprecedented manner to make all people aware of His existence, His mercy, His sovereign rulership, His love for us and His concern for our salvation. There is a God, and He is good. No one can now any longer deny Him unless he chooses to fling the truth back in God's face. The Warning has made God evident. We have felt His power in our bones.

The Warning *shows us our sins.* It was predicted as a "correction of the conscience of the world." The Scriptures foretold long ago that Jesus would send the Holy Spirit to "convict the world of sin." If we did not fully understand before what that meant, we do now, by the power of The Warning. Sin, our resistance to becoming the loving kind of person God is, results in many unloving deeds, decisions, and attitudes. These were all vividly clear in the brilliant light God shone in our souls. Our consciences were thoroughly illuminated at that moment, exposing all the self-deception we are so clever at, pulling out the dead memories that have never been leavened with love, uncovering the lies we told ourselves, the compromises we made. We saw so blatantly the many harsh, stubborn, and unkind decisions we have made, the times we cruelly trod on the feelings of other people, coveted their possessions, envied their good fortune and rejoiced at their failures. Then we groaned with anguish when God revealed to us the neglect, the refusal to help, the undone deeds and the unfulfilled plans. We have heard Him say to us, "Why have you persecuted Me?"

The Warning *was a taste of eternity*. Time stopped for a moment during The Warning, and the truth of timeless existence tumbled in on all of us. It was no longer possible, because of The Warning, to hide from ourselves. All we ever did was before our eyes, seen all at once, in a single glance. We knew then how God's gaze crosses all barriers and grasps the uttermost secrets. He shared with us, for our conversion, how He sees us, and we beheld, in an instant mercifully brief, whatever in us was displeasing to Him. What we understood was our eternal state, should we have died at that time. We suffered for a moment the pain of our sin, the pain of separation from God, the pain of purgatory or hell. God let us see it all, in The Warning.

The Warning was *a mercy from God*. By The Warning we became aware that we are not yet what He wants us to be. We felt the pain of being unlike Him, far from Him. His will is for us to become like Himself, happy in all that He is, and to become close to Him. Sin is the only impediment to that. It prevents us from achieving perfect, even eternal happiness. God unveiled our sinfulness to us in The Warning, not out of revenge, for vengefulness is foreign to His heart, but rather out of love and mercy. He wants us to never have to suffer again the pain we felt in The Warning. His mercy allowed us to sample the pain that sin bequeaths to us. The Warning was truly a mercy from God.

The Warning *is a sign of the future.* It is the major turning-point in world history, the most important "sign of the times." The Warning tells us that all that has gone before in the entire course of world history now focuses on the years just ahead of us. Our age is absolutely critical for the salvation of the human race. A large proportion of all the people who have ever lived are actually living on earth right now. They must have the opportunity to hear and know of God's plan of salvation for them. They need to learn that Jesus has come to take away their sins. All must understand that sin alone deprives us of happiness and the glory of God. Sin is our only real enemy, the only adversary that can destroy us forever. The Warning has prepared all the world's people for the message of the Gospel, prepared them all for Jesus and His life. By The Warning we all know of our sin. We know we need a Saviour. The Warning is the first step for the conversion of the entire world. Without knowing our own sin, we would never understand how much we need Jesus and His forgiveness.

The Warning *is a direct intervention from God.* Never before has God acted directly and universally to make everyone in the world completely aware of their sinfulness before His holiness. The preaching of the Gospel through the witness of the Church has been available for centuries, so it is not as if He had never made such a revelation of this kind before.

But it has not happened in history before that He has acted with such power, such precision, such instancy. The times must be very special. There must not be much time left for repentance. As a race we have repudiated the Gospel message so often and responded to it so sluggishly that what God meant the world to be, in peace, never came to be. The constant pleadings of Mary for us to turn back to God, and her remonstrances over the years while we listened not, are, for believers, sufficient evidence that the present age is even worse than earlier ones. But time is running out. "The times" are about to end, and a new age of peace is promised. The Warning is the first dramatic sign to all that the old age is ending. It is not God's wish that we be among those who refused to repent in time. Not in all the ages is it ever His wish that even a single one of His little ones be lost. For this reason He has intervened, so that the danger would be manifest, the evil of the present age unmasked, and the darkness of false "enlightenment" be exposed. If the world has not wanted to listen to the truth, and the Father's little ones are being misled, He, in His sovereign majesty and power, will compel it to listen. With The Warning, He sweeps away all the sophistry and deception with which Satan has obscured the light of the Gospel.

The Warning *calls us to choose.* We know now, by the grace of The Warning, that each of us has a fateful choice to make. We can choose either to flee from our sin or remain in it. Despite the power of The Warning, we still have our freedom to choose--- we possess a free will. If God took that away from us, we would no longer be human, able to love or to refrain from loving. We have the ability to say

"Yes" or "No," and The Warning confronts us with that responsibility. There is no middle ground. The only choice we have is to be for God or against Him. The situation is just as it was on Mount Carmel, when Elijah called God's people to stand with him and the Lord or with the prophets of Baal and Ashteroth. Like them, we have a choice: choose God, or no-gods; life, or death.

The Warning has made it impossible to delay a decision any longer. To delay is itself a choice for sin. To obtain everlasting life with God we have to amend our lives as disciples of the Lord Jesus, who alone knows the Way to the Father. The alternative is to be lost forever in the pain we fleetingly felt when we knew The Warning. Bliss, or agony---heaven or hell---that is the dilemma. Everything for us depends on which path we select for ourselves.

**The Warning *calls us to prepare for the Miracle.* A "Great Miracle" has been foretold by Our Lady of Mount Carmel, which will happen in the little village of Garabandal. The Warning is a preparation for it, is directly connected with it, and assures us that from the time of The Warning, there will be less than a year's time until the "greatest Miracle the Lord has ever worked for the world" will take place there. A similar, lesser miracle, also predicted in advance, was granted us at Fatima in 1917, in what has come to be known as "The Miracle of the Sun." The sun spun in the sky, and hurtled toward earth. 70,000 spectators saw it happen! Marvelous as that may sound, it is even more wonderful that The Warning has been seen and felt by every inhabitant on the globe! How great indeed is the "Great Miracle" going to be at Garabandal! Millions**

intend to journey there to behold its glory, to be healed there, converted, and comforted. They will travel there because they have known The Warning and been prepared by it to accept The Miracle with faith. The Warning is sending multitudes to that remote Spanish mountain village. It has alerted the entire populace of the earth to the impendng event of The Miracle, and opened hearts to the message and the action of God that will be revealed there.

The news about Fatima took many decades to spread throughout the world. When the "Great Miracle" bursts forth at Garabandal, television, radio, films, newspapers and the countless witnesses viewing The Miracle will spread the story speedily to the farthest corners of the planet. The Warning has prepared us to hear God together at Garabandal, where His people will be gathered once again by God, just as they were on Sinai, to see the fire and the cloud and hear the thunder. By The Warning, God calls the world to the mountain where Our Lady of Mount Carmel appeared in Garabandal. We have been prepared to hear, to heed, and to proclaim the word God will speak to us there.

Finally, we note that *The Warning and The Miracle are inseparable.* They are two aspects of the same intervention of the Lord. Neither can be understood properly without our knowing the other. The Warning prepares for The Miracle, as we have just mentioned, but we can penetrate the mystery of The Warning more profoundly only when we have discovered what The Miracle has to say to us. The Warning has been an extremely painful encounter with the relentless truth of our wretchedness and sin. It needs to be counterbalanced, if we are not to

# Chapter Two

# Review of the Marian Apparitions

## *1830-1986*

### Paris: The Miraculous Medal (1830)

**1**980 marked the 150th anniversary of the first modern appearances of the Blessed Virgin Mary. On July 18th, 1830, to Saint Catherine Labouré, then a young novice of the Sisters of Charity of Saint Vincent De Paul in Paris, Our Lady spoke these telling words: "The times are very evil . . . The whole world will be plunged into every kind of trouble." In that instant she opened to Catherine and to us the long corridor of modern history, wherein so many calamitous events have stricken our globe. By what she said to her, she clearly taught us to connect such misfortunes with our own sinfulness. She had come to call us back to her Son Jesus, away from the darkness. Just as she led Catherine from the sleep of midnight to the chapel where the Light of the World dwelled in the

Eucharist, so she was calling us from our slumber in darkness to new life in the Lord.

Later, she again appeared to Catherine to present her with the image we are familiar with in the "Miraculous Medal." On its face she stands astride the earth in dominion, Satan himself beneath her heel, her hands streaming light upon the world. She said the rays represented graces given by her intercession to those who asked for them. Around the oval perimeter of the image we can read the words,"Oh Mary, conceived without sin, pray for us who have recourse to you." Her victory over evil is signified by this prayer, since her Immaculate Conception is total conquest of sin in a human heart. She leads us into the same victory by her example, and helps us by her prayers to attain it.

In this medal, Mary gave us the outline of the final battle between Satan and the Church which was then about to commence in the historical events of modern times. Already, the Church had been weakened by the darkness of the "Enlightenment" in Europe. The French Revolution had devastated her and torn so many believers from her embrace. Blood was about to flow anew in the streets of Paris in 1830, then again throughout the continent in further revolution (in 1848); and later there was more tribulation in the Franco-Prussian war in 1870, not to mention further conflicts in 1914-1918 (World War I), and more recent disturbances beginning with World War II (1939-1945). Truly the times were very evil, if the pain and sorrow of war is any indication that such was the case.

She came again to a small town called "La-Salette" in Southern France. This time she appeared to two children who were decidedly ungifted, and not particularly religious either. They were herding cattle when she revealed herself in glowing vision, as a sorrowful queen. It was the Feast of Our Lady of Sorrows, September 19th at that period. She was weeping as she moaned to them over the sins of her "children," complaining that she could "no longer hold back the arm of my Son." Dressed in royal fashion, her robes were adorned with the instruments of the Passion, embroidered on her garments in light. In correspondence with her prophecies, a great potato-famine and wheat-blight struck Western Europe, and a convulsive sickness afflicted little children, who died in their mother's arms. In this visitation, her words again clearly assert that the people's sins bring on them such misfortunes. She demands repentance. Her people must obey God and His commandments, or punishment will descend upon them.

## Lourdes: 1858

In 1854, Pius IX defined the dogma of the Immaculate Conception of the Blessed Virgin Mary. Four years later, Bernadette Soubirous, a fourteen-year-old girl whose family was the poorest in Lourdes, France, declared she had seen a Lady in the village dump, where she and two other girls had been gathering firewood. The vision had issued from the heart of a massive rock formation next to the river Gave, in a place called " Massabielle," which literally means "old rock." After several

— 27 —

visits, the Lady asked Bernadette to return fifteen times, which she faithfully did, whereupon she and the whole world received a message and a gift. The message was simple and direct: "Repentance! Repentance! Repentance!" The gift was a beautiful clear spring, coming forth from the base of the rock at a point where Bernadette had obediently dug with her bare hands in the mud, for the Lady had directed that she drink at The Spring. The waters soon displayed miraculous healing properties, and pilgrims began their journeys to Lourdes to bathe in the water and drink at The Spring. Ever since The Spring appeared, countless millions have found living waters at this spot where the Blessed Virgin spoke to a little girl of no account. When Bernadette at last asked the beautiful Lady who she was, the vision confessed, with awesome simplicity, "I am the Immaculate Conception!" Free from sin from the beginning, she showed what the Lord wants for us at the end. Her battle is ours, a fight against sin. If we would only repent of our sins, the calamities that threaten the human race would never occur. There would be the healing and peace that issues from the heart of God, like water from The Rock. Like Mary, we dwell within the "old rock" of the Church, the Rock of Christ. The waters flowing from it in the mystery of Baptism would cleanse us and refresh us with grace.

The miracles at Lourdes continue until today to confront us with the message of Mary and the constant availability of God's healing and forgiveness. The Spring is a reminder that the springs of "living water" are waiting for the people of the world, that they may come and "drink freely, without pay." The weight of sin upon us will be lifted, its stain washed away. The message grows more emphatic with Lourdes. Sin is the core of the problem. The world must change. The Darkness is gathering.

## Fatima: 1917 May 13 to October 13, the thirteenth of each month

Again it is to children that the Virgin reaches out, on this occasion, in Fatima, Portugal. An angel first visits them in 1916, to prepare their hearts to commune with the Mother of God. When the Lady arrives, brighter than the sun in her beauty, she introduces them into the secret of her Immaculate Heart, which she offers as the solution to the problems the world is suffering. In her Heart there is no sin, and therein lies the victory that she predicts, "My Immaculate Heart will triumph!" She points out to the children (and to us) the consequences of sin, and shows them "Hell, where the souls of poor sinners go." This vision displays to their innocent eyes a sea of fire in which they behold the damned. A dire prophecy follows foretelling what will happen on earth if people will not amend their lives: famine, wars and persecutions of the Church and of the Holy Father, the martyrdom of many good people, and even the annihilation of some nations. Russia will continue to spread her errors throughout the world. But, she asserts with authority, "If people will do as I ask, there will be peace." She declared to the children that the peace of the world has been confided into her hands. And, despite what may befall humanity if we refuse to listen, she announces that, "In the end, My Immaculate Heart will triumph, the Holy Father will consecrate Russia to me, Russia will be converted, and an Era of Peace will be given to the world."

Instead of a spring such as she left for us at Lourdes, "Our Lady of the Rosary" (for that is how she identifies herself) promises, months ahead of the event, that on October 13th, at the last appearance, she herself will work a great miracle, "so that all will believe." When the day arrives, 70,000 pilgrims are assembled at the "Cova da Iria," a natural amphitheater seemingly designed for such a spectacle. At noon, sun-time, the clouds part after an all-night rainstorm, and every eye is able to view the sun directly without strain. Shafts of rainbow-like light spin from its orb, dazzling and delighting the onlookers. But suddenly the multitude is appalled as the sun seems to lose its moorings in the heavens; it lurches downward, threatening everyone with obliteration. They are convinced it is the end of the world. Their relief when the sun bounds back to its ordained place in the firmament is beyond expression. But express it they did. There are those still living who were present at that wonder, who continue to render their moving testimony. Not all were professed believers who saw, but even the confirmed skeptics were compelled to speak. The secular and atheistic chronicles of the time recorded in print the witness of those who came to scoff and went home stunned by what had happened at the Cova da Iria.

Fatima is pivotal. It plunges the message of Mary into the sphere of world-wide events. No longer is it only France or some other particular country that receives specific attention. The whole world must listen. In the course of the Second World War, Fatima prophecies were released which, in 1917, had predicted that conflict; soon afterwards the now famous Pilgrim Virgin statues began to travel to every corner of the globe. In the late fifties, the Western World was hearing the message of Fatima from every side. A major motion picture on the subject was distributed. Television programs highlighted the story of Our Lady of Fatima. All waited with anticipation for the "secret" of Fatima to be revealed, for there were tales of a letter sealed with a secret that could not be disclosed until 1960.

By the time the Fatima events had become known throughout the Catholic world, the Second World War was already in progress. No further proof of their authenticity was necessary, for that war had been foretold as a punishment, and we were right in the middle of it. It was clear that we were not amending our lives according to her requests. There was not enough response in prayer and penance to bring about the peace Our Lady of the Rosary had promised, "If people do as I ask." Peace had not come. The war ended with the explosion of two mighty bombs which introduced us into the nuclear age of annihilation. The situation was deteriorating rather than improving, and the moral fabric of society began to disintegrate badly. Great fissures opened up between the "Third World" and the rich nations, and Communism continued to "spread her errors throughout the world."

What did the "Secret of Fatima" contain? The curiosity of so many was disappointed when Pope John XXIII, according to the story, opened the sealed letter from Lucy (the sole remaining visionary of Fatima) in 1960, and chose not to reveal what was written in it. Just a year previously he had announced, on January 25, 1959, the convocation of an Ecumenical Council at the Vatican. As this history-making gathering of the world's bishops unfolded, the Fatima "secret" was gradually forgotten, and somehow, despite the solemn exhortation of the Council Fathers to maintain devotion to the Mother of God, and even though Pope Paul VI proclaimed her as *"Mother of the Church"* (with the immediate acclamation of the Council), not only did devotion to the Blessed Mother decline; a general disappearance of expressed love for her ensued, as changes in theology, liturgy, and devotional practice flowed from the Council.

### Garabandal: 1961

Lucy of Fatima has testified that Our Lady appeared to her a "seventh time" at the Cova da Iria, where the sun had whirled in the sky. Our Lady of the Rosary was fulfilling a promise she had made to her during the apparitions in 1917, when there were the three of them, Lucy, Francisco, and Jacinta. But now the latter two had gone "to heaven," as the Lady had promised they would, and Lucy was leaving Fatima for school and a new life. She visited each of the sacred places where they had met their heavenly visitors, the Angel of Peace and Our Lady. It was night, and that very morning, before the sun rose, she would leave Fatima for good. When she at last reached the "Cova", Our Lady kept her promise. Lucy saw her there a seventh time. It was June 18th, 1921.

Forty years later to the very day, on the evening of June 18th, 1961, the apparitions of Garabandal began. As at Fatima and Paris, an angel prepared the way. In this case he identified himself as Saint Michael the Archangel. Soon Our Lady of Mount

Carmel arrived, on July 2nd, the Feast of the Visitation.

It was time to remind us of the message again. After forty years of tumult in history and in the life of the Church, Fatima was failing to keep the interest of the new generation. Our Lady of Mount Carmel repeats herself with dramatic intensity in a little village in the hill country of Spain. She calls these "the last warnings," and foretells catastrophe if, in this, the final hour, the world still refuses to listen.

The Garabandal apparitions continued for four years in a great profusion of phenomena never seen before in previous visitations she had made. At last the visions became less frequent, until they ceased in 1965. A final message was given in that year to the world, again on that mysterious date, June 18th. Some estimate that during those years there were about 2000 meetings between Our Lady of Mount Carmel and the four young seers: Conchita, Loli, Jacinta, and Mary Cruz. The Lady was very beautiful, according to their reports, and quite motherly, kissing the children on each occasion that she visited them, especially whenever she bid them goodbye. She taught them to pray, guiding them in the recitation of the Rosary, chided them about their conduct, chatted and played with them as a mother with her young children, and she even allowed them to play with the Infant Jesus, whom she frequently carried with her. She affirmed in various ways those doctrines and devotions that would shortly come under attack or be abandoned, such as the devotion to herself that had long been traditional, love for the Eucharist and visits to the Blessed Sacrament, the importance of prayer, the validity and power of blessings, particularly of religious articles, which she kissed and gave back to their owners to take home. She also stressed the importance of frequent, even daily reception of Holy Communion, the power and dignity of priests and the Mass, the necessity of obedience to Church authority (emphasized as a key point), and belief in and reliance on the ministry of angels and saints. Above all, she repeated the injunction to repent of our sins and seek forgiveness, especially in confession. She recommended we perform much penance, and make many sacrifices. She said we should sacrifice ourselves more. She warned of punishment to come, worse than any that had yet been experienced, if we did not amend our lives.

Many all over the world received the faith to believe in the visions and the message of Garabandal, and sincerely reformed their lives. The religious articles carried from town to town after having been "kissed" by the vision wrought healings and conversions.

For those who felt Our Lady's kiss touch them in the power of her love, the reality of the appearances and the importance of the message have never been in doubt.

But Our Lady of Mount Carmel had also revealed that confusion would assail the Church, and that "in the end, few would believe." This statement of hers seems to have been amply fulfilled at the time we are writing this book (1982). It appears that all the visitations and the messages of Mary have been practically forgotten or are ignored by most Catholics, including the clergy. Until The Warning struck us, confronting us relentlessly with the truth of her words, we seem to have put them all aside as past and pointless history.

The Warning pulls the veil of Satan's deception away from our eyes. God now *demands* that we listen. Up to now we have not chosen to do so, especially when Mary has called on us to change our lives. The Warning is God's mercy to us, showing us that we must change, we must repent, we must listen --- or we perish.

The finality of the Garabandal series of apparitions is underlined by her words to the visionaries, "You are now in the last warnings!" Garabandal recapitulates all the previous Marian apparitions as it focuses in on the "end of the times." Her self-designation there as *Our Lady of Mount Carmel* digs back into history over 730 years to her meeting with Saint Simon Stock. She gave him the Brown Scapular, since then a traditional symbol associating salvation with her protection. Guadalupe (Mexico: 1531) presents her as the one who crushes the serpent's head. Her intercession releases grace for world conversion. The Miraculous Medal given in 1830 depicts her as "Mary, conceived without sin," and again recommends seeking graces from her intercession in order to battle the sinful times we were then entering. La-Salette in 1846, Lourdes in 1858, Fatima in 1817 each explicitly identify sin as the source of the "troubles" the Virgin predicted to Saint Catherine Labouré would afflict the "whole world." When she begins to appear again at Garabandal, she reminds us of all the lessons she taught in foregoing ages, and then applies them precisely to current evils soon to infect the Church's life. The high point of these encounters at the tiny mountain village of Garabandal is a mid-night rendezvous in 1962 between Conchita and the Archangel Michael, who gives her Holy Communion in the street, in pitch darkness. It is July 18th, 1962, the very anniversary of Saint Catherine Labouré's first visit with the Blessed Virgin in 1830. The Eucharist is visible on her extended tongue and luminous, so that the bystanders, huddled around her in the dark, can see the miraculous host. Again Mary reiterates the teaching that the Eucharist is the light that conquers the darkness engulfing the world, repeating what had been indicated to Saint Catherine Labouré, brought to the altar in the brightly illuminated chapel at midnight.

# TOMORROW

# Chapter Three

# The Miracle

Since we have not yet experienced The Miracle, we know only what the Blessed Virgin told us about it. She has revealed enough for us to prepare for this world-shaking occurrence, which will take place at Garabandal within a year of The Warning. We can therefore expect it to happen soon, since we have already felt and seen The Warning. The Miracle is only a short time away from us.

Its exact date is not known, except by Conchita, who knows the day, the date, and the year. She has been forbidden by the Blessed Virgin to disclose it until eight days before it is to happen. At that moment she will announce it to the whole world. She has never revealed the date to anyone.

For twenty years we have waited for the "greatest miracle the Lord has ever worked for the world," during which "the sick" who are at the site "will be cured" and the "unbelievers will be converted." This long waiting-period strikingly distinguishes Garabandal from Fatima, where the predicted miracle of the sun was worked during the course of those apparitions. Also, there was no promise of wholesale healing and conversion at Fatima, but at Garabandal this promise is made.

*Only one person has seen The Miracle*, in vision. His name was Father Luis Andreu, a Jesuit seminary professor who came to the village in 1961 less than a week before the Feast of the Assumption. He never returned home from his visit to examine the situation. He was unexpectedly swept into the children's vision of Our Lady, and then caught up by himself into the experience of the coming Miracle. Of course, this convinced him of the authenticity of the apparitions. His heart was so full of joy that it overcame him. On the way back to the seminary, in the early morning hours of the next day, he quietly expired. He did not live to describe The Miracle.

The Blessed Virgin assured the children that "nothing bad would happen" on the day of The Miracle. Presumably this is an assurance that no one else will die from seeing it, as Father Luis did. But his experience of such joy and the remarks he made afterwards about what he saw, taken together with statements by the other visionaries which repeat what Mary told them about The Miracle, reveals that it will be a glorious manifestation of God's love and mercy for us all.

*Millions will be able to see it on that day*, for Garabandal is perched among hills forming a broad natural amphitheater well able to accommodate the vast multitude which will journey to that remote place when it happens. Somehow, depite the fairly primitive circumstances, their needs will be provided for. A great assembly will converge on the village from everywhere, and all who manage to reach its environs will behold the same vision of joy that sent Father Luis to heaven.

The Miracle *will be a revelation*. The Marian visitations, like biblical events, are revelatory in every respect. They convey a message, not only in the verbal communications of the Mother of God, but in the events themselves, the persons involved, the circumstances, the surroundings. The symbolism, for instance, of The Spring at Lourdes obviously presents a Baptismal message, a revelation that reinforces the Church's teaching on that Sacrament. God's healing power is clearly evident in the many miracles that occur at the grotto. The Rock of Lourdes is the Church in which Mary dwells and from which the living waters flow, giving life to the whole world. Study of the Marian events uncovers so much meaning hidden away in what at first glance may appear inconsequential.

The Miracle *will be a clear revelation of God's mercy*. We must prepare ourselves for this, so that when it happens we will fully grasp its significance and absorb its power. Even now we can begin to meditate fruitfully on the information already offered us by Our Lady about The Miracle. These hints are for our benefit, so that we will be more ready to fully appreciate The Miracle when it happens.

The Miracle *will be Eucharistic*. The emphasis on devotion to the Most Holy Eucharist is so strong at Garabandal that a Eucharistic theme for The Miracle would be in perfect consonance with everything that happened in the village during the apparitions. We can also expect a Eucharistic event because it has been revealed that The Miracle will take place at 8:30 on a Thursday evening (about the same time as the Last Supper), and that on the day of The Miracle the Church will be celebrating the Feast of a young Martyr of the Eucharist. We must be ready to receive an unmistakable proof from God, through The Miracle, that the Holy Eucharist is the center of our life in the Church, and that Jesus is truly present to us in the Eucharist, in His living Flesh. We are to avail ourselves of this Sacrament as frequently as we can.

The Miracle *will be ecclesial*, that is, it will support the truth that through the Body of Christ which is the Church, Head and members, all graces come, and that all men and women are called not only to follow Jesus personally, but also to enter His Church and to submit to its discipline, teaching and sacraments. For this reason, The Miracle will happen in connection with a "great ecclesiastical event." God's timing is the Church's timing, and the Church's authority will be reinforced and authenticated by the fact that the "ecclesiastical event" and The Miracle will occur on the same day, perhaps at the very same instant. Also, the Pope, the visible Head of the Church, will see The Miracle from wherever he is.

The Miracle *will be Marian*, that is, it will in some way so assert the glory of the Mother of God that all Christians will know that God is commanding that they give up their objections to her role in the Body of Christ and that they pay her the honor that God Himself gives her. The message of Fatima will be brought into high relief, namely, that only when the world gives the Immaculate Heart of Mary the honor and devotion due her, and only when we consecrate our hearts to that Heart as individuals and as nations, will peace at last spread through the world. Through this great Miracle, all will learn to love "Holy Mary, Mother of God."

The Miracle *will convert the whole world.* This assertion was made by Our Lord Himself to Conchita. He answered a question of hers about Russia's conversion by assuring her that The Miracle was not only for the "conversion of Russia," but "for the conversion of the whole world," and that "thus, all will love our hearts"(the hearts of Jesus and Mary). It would seem by His words that somehow the Miracle will show us all how closely the hearts of Jesus and Mary are united, as a symbol of the kind of peace-giving love that should unite our hearts. Perhaps the two hearts on the reverse side of the "Miraculous Medal" were a prophecy as well as a lesson, foretelling an age ahead where all hearts will be reconciled as are the hearts of Jesus and Mary. Reconciliation of hearts is what conversion is all about, and it would seem that all the Marian appearances concern themselves with it. God wants to unite all hearts in His Church. The Miracle will make that plain to everyone, and it will summon us together from the four winds to make it clear that we belong to each other. By the power of The Miracle, we will be bound together in the same fiery love that forges perfect communion between the hearts of Jesus and Mary.

The Miracle *will be sacramental.* The healings and conversions at Garabandal will come through experiencing The Miracle. It will not be just a spectacle---something to look at and talk about when we return home. The Miracle will be *filled with power*, and we who are fortunate enough to behold it will take power home with us. We will be like the witnesses at Pentecost. God will send us home to tell people all over the world of the great mercy and love that He has for us. We will be transformed by the graces of The Miracle into apostles filled with the Holy Spirit, bold with a message that is crucial for the world's salvation.

The Miracle *will be a warning*. Once The Miracle happens, the human race must change, or face the most terrible catastrophe the world has ever seen: *The Punishment*. Blessing as The Miracle will be, it will make evident, even if only by the fact that it will be so stupendous, that this is our last chance.There will not be another miracle like this one. It will be very great because of the great needs of the world. But this time, unless the people heed the message, The Punishment will surely come. Even though an "Era of Peace" finally awaits us, unless the people amend their lives now, The Punishment will come. There will be no escape from it. The Miracle will have set the fuse. Unless we extinguish its burning by repentance, *The Punishment will come*.

The Miracle *will be for the glory of God*. God's glory is in our knowing Him as He is, and in our turning to Him in love. We will experience His glory in The Miracle, for we will know His mercy, His unmeasured love for us, His goodness. He who did not spare His only Son for us will let us understand His tender and most merciful love, through The Miracle. It will remind us of all His promises to forgive, to heal, to raise from the dead and to glorify us with His glory. We will also see how wonderful a Mother we have in Mary, and behold how marvelously the glory of God shines in her Assumption. We will comprehend the glory of God in the Church, signified in the people gathered around the mountain in Garabandal. When we return from the mountain, we shall have seen the glory of the Lord, and be eager to sound His glory to all the others. The glory of Sion, the glory of the New Pentecost prayed for by Pope John XXIII as he opened the Second Vatican Council and again by Pope Paul VI when he drew it to a close, will flow over the whole Church and the entire world. "And thus," as Jesus revealed to Conchita, "all will love our hearts."

earth by removing sinners themselves from it. By His patient delay of the drastic surgery implied in The Punishment, He mercifully gives more time to those who are "on their way to perdition," but He cannot wait any longer, since it has become evident that their hearts are so hardened that the Holy Spirit will never be able to convert them. Since the danger is very great that if their course is not terminated they will "take many souls with them," then, "for the sake of the elect, the time will be shortened," and The Punishment will come to them to take them away.

God could have acted in such a manner at any time in history if He wished. There is even an Old Testament story describing how the world became so sinful that God "repented" that He had made men, and He sent a flood that drowned everyone except His faithful servant, Noe, and his family, and animals of every kind. It teaches the people of God that there is a limit to the lawlessness and degradation that the Lord will permit. God is holy and He is sovereign ruler; all creation must acknowledge Him. We must live according to His commandments, otherwise we will destroy ourselves and encounter the mysterious "wrath" of God.

Perhaps, with The Punishment, the story of Noe will acquire an apocalyptic significance that the author never envisioned, for The Punishment, like the Flood, may come upon an unheeding and scornful world to destroy its evil, while those who have cleansed their heart of sin and trusted in the Lord's mercy will be saved.

The survivors of The Punishment will be protected by the Lord for the Era of Peace, when the dove of the Holy Spirit will announce to us that the flood of wickedness has passed, and we can begin to live life anew, in the time of conversion when "all will love Our Hearts." In the Hearts of Jesus and Mary, all men and women on earth will learn to be faithful, and they will fill the earth with love.

The Punishment *will be the last* of the punishments before the Era of Peace. God's work to bring the world to Himself will be done. Before the Gospel could be "preached to all the nations" "wars and rumors of wars" had to come, and many other calamities take place. The Warning and The Miracle had to happen to show the whole world that Jesus is Lord, so that all would abandon the errors which up to now have kept so many from embracing the Gospel and the Church. Only by The Warning, The Miracle, and either the threat of, or actual infliction of, the Punishment, could the world, the whole world, be made ready for the acceptance of the Good News of Jesus and His Way. For one hundred and fifty years the Mother of God had shown us that our afflictions were connected with our sins; we were being "punished " for them, both in this life and the next. The Punishment, if it comes, will be the utterly convincing evidence that her words have been true all along. There will no longer be any need for further punishment from God. The Punishment will effect a transformation of the world that will forever alter history. It will no longer be the way it was. The whole world will worship God and His Son Jesus Christ, come into the Church, and live lives worthy of Him. An era, a "certain period" of peace, will be given to the world.

The Punishment *will not be the end of the world, nor will it be a war.* The Blessed Virgin told the visionaries of Garabandal that The Punishment will not be a war. It will be directly from God. It will not be humanity's own doing. But The Punishment cannot mean the end of the world either, since there is an unconditional promise from Our Lady of Fatima that a "certain period of peace" will be given to the world after the Triumph of her Immaculate Heart, the consecration of Russia to that Heart, and Russia's conversion. Conchita did state that we would know, when we experience The Warning, that we would be entering into the end of time. But that may not mean the end of time is very near in human estimation, nor would necessarily imply that The Punishment itself will end time. After all, the Era of Peace is surely coming. Perhaps her statement might better be interpreted to mean that The Warning, The Miracle, and The Punishment will together usher in the final age of the world.

*No one will escape The Punishment,* as none of us escaped The Warning. Directly from God, it will encompass everyone. Both the bad and the good will suffer, for in some way we are all tainted by sin. The Punishment will invade every corner of the planet. Many will die, and Our Lady recommends that all should beg God's forgiveness, and that all Catholics should go to confession. Obviously this means that when The Punishment is imminent, there will still be time for all to confess. We will know beforehand that it is coming. All should be ready to enter eternity in God's grace, should they suffer death in The Punishment.

The Punishment will not therefore be so selective as was, for instance, the punishment of God in Egypt on the first-born, when the sons of the Egyptians died and those of the Israelites were "passed over." In The Punishment, both good and bad will die. No indication whatsoever is given about how many, or what proportion of the world's population will survive. But the coming of the "Era of Peace"afterwards assures us that some of us will pass through the fire of The Punishment unharmed. It would seem that the ones who are spared, whether they heeded The Warning and The Miracle or not, will certainly be finally converted by the trial of The Punishment. Every person who emerges from it alive will have no alternative but a new life. The old world will be gone. The results of the world's sinfulness will appear so abhorrent that people will want to reject sin completely. A New Pentecost will then become possible. The Era of Peace will blossom, the goodness of the Immaculate Heart of Mary will flourish in every heart in "triumph." The whole world will come into a reunited Church, and all nations will be at peace. If The Punishment comes, no one will escape it, but neither will anyone who lives after it fail to share the blessed peace that will renew the world.

# Chapter Five

# The Permanent Sign

**W**e have not yet mentioned in this book The Permanent Sign that the Blessed Virgin promised would remain at Garabandal after The Miracle at "The Pines" (a grove of nine pines outside the village at the top of a rocky lane leading up the hill). Little has been revealed about the nature of this Sign. We know the following details: it will remain at The Pines until the end of the world; we will be able to see, photograph, and televise it, but not touch it; no one will be able to explain it by scientific analysis (it will be supernatural). *It will remind us forever* of the Great Miracle, which will center on that very spot. Anyone who wishes will be able to go to Garabandal after The Miracle and examine The Sign. It will recall to our minds that God summons the world to repentance, and testify throughout time that the Lord insists that we abandon our sins. Because it will remain there until the world ends, it will also insist by its presence that the world will indeed one day end, and that Jesus will come again on the "clouds of heaven" "to make all things new," and to "judge the living and the dead."

The Warning, the Miracle, and The Punishment must be taken as a single redemptive event in order to be understood. *The Sign will be a reminder of all three of them.* People will remember what happened, and will tell their children and grandchildren of the great deeds of God that transpired there. After The Miracle, this Sign will begin its work, while the populace of the globe is passing through the period of challenge to conscience The Miracle will induce. The Sign will be there in the midst confronting us, crying out by its very presence: "Repentance!" as did Our Lady of Lourdes. It will not let us forget that The Punishment will surely come if The Warning and The Miracle are ignored.

The Sign will focus our attention on the truth that *God has visibly intervened on this mountain,* just as He did on Mount Sinai and Mount Calvary, on Mount Carmel, and at Pentecost on Mount Sion ---to call His people to Himself. Patriarchs of old set up altars and monuments to commemorate forever their experience of God at a certain place, which then became forever sacred by His coming. At Garabandal, for the first time in history, the Lord Himself sets His own Sign in The Pines for a perpetual memorial of His saving act for today's world.

*The Sign calls us all to holiness.* The Israelites were continually reminded by the fiery cloud hovering over The Meeting Tent that God was with them, leading them relentlessly to holiness and to the Holy Land. The Sign will be with us like that cloud of God's glory, to remind us that the Lord is leading us also to holiness and to the land of heaven, and that He will not tolerate idolatry among His people. There is only One God, and Jesus, born of

Mary, is His Only-begotten Son. We must follow Him back to the Father; there is no other Way. We are to climb the mountain of Calvary He climbed, just as Moses once climbed up Mount Sinai into the fiery cloud. With Jesus, the new Moses, and in Him, we enter the cloud and fire, to meet God "face-to-Face." The Sign will be high on the mountain, in Garabandal, a mountain often shrouded in clouds just above The Pines. The Sign will beckon to us all: "Come to The Mountain, where God dwells." Whoever journeys there will be touched by the power in the cloud, the same power that can send The Warning, The Miracle, and The Punishment. The Sign will interpret history to the generation that beholds it, saying, "There is only One God, and Jesus is His Son. Do not again worship false gods, else punishment will come again." If we are tempted to go to war again, to again choose values and actions that are selfish and sinful rather than choose God, then The Sign will be there to warn us that such will be the way of death. It will be a permanent "warning" of what could happen again, should we reject Him. The Sign will make the place holy over which it blazes, calling us to holiness.

*The Sign will point to heaven.* It will tell us always that this present life will one day end, and that we will ascend, as Jesus and Mary did, to an eternal life that is beyond the clouds and our understanding. Our destiny is to live forever with God in heaven. The permanence of The Sign will persuade us to keep our eyes fixed, not on earthly, but on heavenly things. Its presence in the center of a renewed world will demand the holiness that heaven knows. We must prevent what happened before from happening again, by avoiding sin and embracing heaven's holy way. The Sign will recall to us that it was because of sin that the former world was destroyed and rejected. It will continue to alert us, as The Warning once did to the world at large, of the terrible danger that sin presents to our lives and happiness. It will cast light on our sin and show it to be the true enemy that it is: sin alone can deprive us of heaven.

*The Sign will guard the "Era of Peace."* The period of peace that Our Lady promised at Fatima will come. The duration of that peace is indefinite; she assures us that we will be given a "certain period" of peace. The Peace can be squandered by sin. In none of Mary's prophecies does she predict that sin will cease after God intervenes. The struggle against sin will continue, even until the Day of the Lord when Jesus comes again to wipe it out forever. As children are being born who have never known the previous age and its degradation, nor The Warning, The Miracle, or The Punishment, they, like all others before them, will be tempted by sin. The Sign will instruct them, reinforcing the teaching of their parents, that they must never sin as their forebears did. Otherwise The Peace they have inherited will be lost again, and then surely people would destroy one another and bring a final end to the world. These children and their children in turn will be able to go to Garabandal to gaze on The Sign --- a testimony against the sins of past generations, an explanation of why the old world had to end and why there is now peace and unity, and a warning for the future, that never again must men and women  offend our Lord so much.The children of today's generation will return home chastened by the sight of The Permanent Sign and by its power, for somehow it will enlighten their minds and fire their hearts to know their own sinfulness, and call them to repentance too, purifying them as they come near its glory. The Sign will protect the Era of Peace by commanding each one to be at peace with brother and sister, with self and with God. It will guard the age to come until the end of the world.

# THE
# NEXT
# DAY

# Chapter
## Six

# The Triumph of the
# Immaculate Heart

**"My** *Immaculate Heart will triumph!"* This prophecy of Our Lady of Fatima, unlike most of the others, is unconditional; it will come to pass, and nothing will prevent it from happening. The Triumph is a certainty. To achieve it is the very purpose for which the Mother of God has been visiting and importuning us for so long a time. "In the end," she assures us, " My Immaculate Heart will triumph." At the climax of the battle between good and evil, between the Church (Mary especially) and the Dragon (Satan and his followers), goodness will be totally triumphant over wickedness. The struggle will be over. The Evil One will be defeated, his head crushed by her heel. The Woman shall conquer.

*The meaning of The Triumph is victory over sin.* In Mary's own Heart, good has already triumphed absolutely. There is no sin in her. She is already glorified in heaven, untouched in any way by evil's contamination. Victory over evil has reached its zenith in her Immaculate Heart. The coming of The Triumph of that Heart, however, must signify more than her own personal triumph. The prophecy refers to her triumph happening in us, as sin is cast out through repentance, and love reigns in the world. In The Triumph, our hearts will become like hers.

Her Triumph *is victory over evil in our own hearts*. This is what happens at the moment of our conversion from sin. The Triumph of the Immaculate Heart takes hold when a heart turns toward God with Mary's faith and surrender. When we say "Yes" to God, declaring our "fiat" as she did, The Triumph begins in us. She allowed God to be all in her. As God's messenger, she invites us to accept the saving power of God calling us to repentance. Our triumph begins when we say "Yes" to Him, and it grows and puts down roots more deeply until that Day when we will be raised up with Christ, just as Mary was raised up in her Assumption. The Triumph will appear on earth, "in the end," when everyone in the world consents to repeat the "Yes" of Mary given to God when she consented to become Mother to His Holy One, Jesus.

The Triumph *has already begun*, therefore, because many, the world over, have already listened to the Marian messages over the years, and have made the choices she asked for. They have said "Yes" to the Lord, and joined with Mary in prayer and sacrifice to help save us all and bring the Era of Peace. In some, this triumph of a faith-filled "Yes" has been in their hearts for many years, even from childhood. The prayers and virtuous lives of these people have certainly brought blessing and protection to an undeserving generation. But for the vast majority, The Triumph seems to have not yet begun. It is to these children of hers that the Blessed Mother directs her appeals. She does not want them to be lost. They must and will turn to the Lord and be saved. In them also, The Triumph will come.

By her prophecy quoted above, the Queen of Heaven assures us that *the present situation will be reversed by the intervention of God.* By His great mercy, by the intercession of the Immaculate Heart and of those who join with her in her efforts to turn the world around, it will happen. Not only Russia, but the whole world will be converted. Mary has promised that conversion; The Warning we have recently known imperiously demands it. The Miracle soon to be seen in Garabandal has world-conversion as its purpose. The Punishment, if it comes, will guarantee it. The conversion of the world is sure to come. The world will become His by our conversion and His intervention. The Triumph of the Immaculate Heart will arrive.

The Triumph *will glorify Mary, the Mother of God.* God "wishes to establish in the world devotion to the Immaculate Heart." He wills to glorify His Mother on earth. His intention in this regard is obvious when we consider the implications of her Assumption, a mystery which assures us that He has already given to her personally all the glory she can receive. He fills her with glory through Jesus, her Son, who has that glory as His very own. He who is "full of grace and of truth," the "Only-begotten of the Father" "on whom His favor rests," wants to glorify His own Mother to the utmost, by giving to her the fullness of Resurrection that He himself has received from the Holy Spirit.

We are to support Him in this enterprise. We glorify Mary with Him. We must acknowledge before all men and women the marvelous work He has accomplished in her, making her more beautiful than the sun and stars, more comely than the moon, crowning her Queen of all in the dazzling raiment of the Lord's light.

We will glorify her by obeying her perennial summons to repentance, by imitating her response to Jesus, by proclaiming her name as *Mother of God and Mother of the Church*. God wants it to be known the world over that the triumph of good over evil is meant to come, and certainly will come, through her Immaculate Heart. She will be glorified by both God and us on earth, for it will become manifest that God has worked The Triumph through her.

The Triumph *will be a conversion event* that will be so powerful and universal that all will be compelled to praise God for the magnificent works He has done in His creature, Mary. The awesome might that this humble handmaiden possesses as she shares in the redemption of the world will be abundantly clear before all eyes. The Triumph will be recognizable in the total conversion of the world —an historical event of such magnitude that it will make all former moments of glory seem like shadows. God will accord immense glory to Mary, the Immaculate Heart, and we will then begin to comprehend with what glory He intends to adorn each of us, in our turn. Mary will show forth, in her Triumph, the inestimable glory promised to the Church (to each one of us). Our destiny is the same as hers, if we repent of our sins and seek the Lord with our whole heart. We too will be glorified by God with Jesus and Mary, and with the same glory of the Holy Spirit they have received from the Father.

from others. Saint Bernadette went through excruciating agonies of body and mind in the last
years of her short life. The children of Fatima suffered not only during the apparitions, but afterwards also. Jacinta and Francisco both embraced
self-imposed penances which Our Lady approved,
but which were very difficult indeed. Both of these
little ones suffered terrible physical pain because of
the diseases to which they eventually succumbed,
first Francisco, then Jacinta. Our Lady took them
to heaven, which she had promised to do, but not
without their first enduring much suffering "for sinners." She had asked them on her first meeting with
them whether they were willing to accept all the suffering God would send them for the conversion of
sinners and in reparation for sin. All three had
answered "Yes." To this Our Lady rejoined, "Then
you will have much to suffer, but the grace of God
will be your comfort." And so it happened. When
she returned later to announce to them that the
First World War would soon end because of their
prayers, they knew they had hastened the peace.
But it was prayer, penance, and reparation that had
turned the tide of evil, not the arms and might of men.

None of the messages given to the visionaries is
for themselves alone. They, in their experiences
with their heavenly visitor, always in some way
represent us. Some of the suffering they endure is
exceptional, to make the point that suffering has
meaning and power---power to redeem the world.
We ought to understand this simply by our looking
intently at Jesus crucified on the Cross, but we seem
to need reminding that the lesson applies to our suf-
ferings as well. We, the members of the Body of
Christ Jesus, like the children of Fatima and the

others who saw Our Lady, are called into the penance and reparation which can hasten The Triumph and bring peace to the world.

*Daily duty is penance and reparation.* Our Lord told Lucy of Fatima some years after the apparitions that the penance He now seeks and requires of us is that we embrace *the daily duties before us.* He demands nothing unusual, but only that we accept fully the discipline daily duty entails, and the pain it includes. Such fidelity will hasten The Triumph, since it puts into practice what has happened in the heart. We can pray and be converted interiorly, but our conversion must emerge in the fulfillment of daily duty and in responsible behaviour. Love is not love until it is expressed in a human way. It must be visible in our relationships with others, if it is to become real.

There is considerable penance in our lives when we apply ourselves to daily duty. We need not look far from the demands of every-day life to discover self-sacrifice and love. The will of the Father is hidden in the ordinary responsibilities of each day. Not even Jesus Himself performed any special penance that we know of. He simply accomplished His Father's will, going about doing good. For His efforts, He was crucified, and by His pain He redeemed the world. So it is with all of us. The children of Fatima were not asked by the Lady, "Will you please choose the hardest penance you can think of, to make reparation for the sins of the world?", but rather, "Will you accept all the suffering God will *send* you?' Into every person's life God sends suffering. The events and circumstances of each day point out to us the path of love God wishes us to follow. Our acts of penance and reparation are tied up in the little things, seemingly insignificant, that tug on us moment-by-moment, saying to us: "This way to love; that way to love." The will of the Father is evident if we are willing to embrace love and the pain it includes. Doing the Father's will in love is the perfect method to hasten "The Triumph of the Immaculate Heart and the Era of Peace."

*Amendment of life will hasten The Triumph.* "Men must amend their lives," Our Lady of Fatima declared. "They must stop offending Our Lord, who is already too much offended." We must give up sin and become imitators of Jesus and Mary if we are to bring about The Triumph sooner. Amendment of life is the central condition of the world's renewal. Unless we amend and change our lives, no amount of praying or penance will bring the Era of Peace. There will be no peace, no triumph, until we reform. The failure to heed this challenge is the reason why The Warning has finally confronted us. Sin threatens us with catastrophe. Sin must be abandoned. We must keep God's commandments and give up our wayward, selfish deeds. Destruction threatens our civilization, our security, our very lives. "Certain nations will be annihilated" if the present situation does not change. Amendment of life is the most determinative element in God's program to save us from disaster. More swiftly than anything else we can do, true repentance will avert The Punishment and hasten The Triumph. We must amend our lives, "for Our Lord is already too much offended."

*Consecration to the Immaculate Heart will hasten*

*The Triumph.* To amend our lives so radically, however, is like moving a mountain. Surely this is why the Lord wants to establish in the world Devotion to the Immaculate Heart of Mary. She proclaimed, "To those who embrace this devotion I promise salvation." Devotion to her Heart will bring us the graces we need to thoroughly amend our lives. We need to seriously consider how to embrace this devotion and remain faithful to it. It assures our own victory over the sin within us. Our being devoted to her Immaculate Heart will hasten the world-wide Triumph over evil which has been prophesied by Our Lady of Fatima.

### —IMPORTANT NOTE—

The next chapter of this little book deserves special attention.

In the final vision of Fatima Our Lady appeared as Our Lady of Mt. Carmel (as she appeared at Garabandal) holding the Brown Scapular of Carmel out to the world.

When Lucia was asked why this apparition of Our Lady of Mt. Carmel with the Scapular she replied:

*"Because She wants everyone to wear it. It is the sign of consecration to Her Immaculate Heart."*

In the next chapter Fr. Bebie explains the meaning of this consecration realized through the Scapular Devotion without going into details about the Scapular itself. For further information we urge the reader to consult a classic book on this subject titled *Sign of Her Heart,* published by AMI Press, Washington, NJ 07882 . . . also a new book soon to appear: *Her Glorious Title.*

Chapter
Eight

# Consecration and Devotion to the Immaculate Heart

*C onsecration is a form of devotion.* Devotion to the Immaculate Heart can be embraced in a variety of ways, but the one that seems most appropriate today is "consecration." Our Lady of Fatima asked for the consecration of Russia to her Immaculate Heart, and promised that this would bring about that country's conversion. Consecration is immensely powerful, capable of bringing down graces from heaven that render impossible things possible. In the light of the prophecy about Russia's conversion through consecration, a multitude of Catholics have chosen to consecrate themselves to Mary's Immaculate Heart, thereby expressing in the most adequate way they know their devotion to that Heart. Even though individual consecration was not demanded by Our Lady in any of her apparitions, it would nonetheless appear to be the most complete method to express "devotion" to her Immaculate Heart, and to live that devotion out in everyday life. Those consecrated to her are decided in their own hearts to be continually devoted to her and to carry out her requests. Consecration is the Triumph of the Immaculate Heart happening in their hearts.

The consecrated heart is dedicated to becoming like Mary's Immaculate Heart: sinless, full of love. Those who live their consecration witness to The Triumph already realized in them. *They have made the choice to allow themselves to be converted.* They follow Jesus without reservation. They invited others to the same whole-hearted self-giving to the Lord. Their hearts reflect the goodness and kindness of Mary's Heart. The Immaculate Heart of Mary, the perfect response to Jesus, becomes visible in the lives of those consecrated to that Heart.*

For these reasons, all should seriously consider *consecrating themselves to the Immaculate Heart personally.* Those who have already done so can testify to consecration's quiet transforming power. They sense that because they have commended themselves completely into the protecting arms of their Mother, she is continually present to them in a new way. They know they are receiving graces they would otherwise not have, because their Mother, Mary Immaculate, is looking after them. They allow her to be for them what God wants her to be. They rely on her acting in them as Mother and Queen. They know her in a new way because of their consecration, and they understand that being devoted to her Immaculate Heart will be the assurance of their salvation.

*Consecration is a simple matter.* We hand over our whole being into the mystery of being mothered

*This is a beautiful explanation of the devotion of the Scapular of Mt. Carmel. See the book: *Sign of Her Heart,* AMI Press, Washington, NJ 07882.

by Mary. In this we imitate Jesus, who, as a little infant, was hers, and who never revoked this gift of Himself to her. We say "Yes" to Mary as He did. We believe God works powerfully through her, and that we are surrendering to that power as it comes through her Heart. Consecration can be expressed most concisely by affirming that it is the same as saying "Yes" to Mary, the Immaculate Heart, just as she is, and just as God gives her to us. We accept the gift of her that Jesus made to us when He said from the Cross to the "beloved disciple," "This is your Mother." We "take her into our own," that is, into everything we have and are.

We attribute no more to her, and no less, than God himself does. Since He made her His Mother, we acknowledge this. We allege also that she is our Mother because He gave her to us when He died on the Cross. She reigns with Him; we let her reign over us. She is sinless, and we aspire to be sinless too. She is full of love and we want to be like her. We consecrate ourselves to all these truths about Mary as we consecrate ourselves to her person. We relate to her just as God has revealed her to be, and we hold back from her none of the glory that God Himself has granted her.

*Consecration opens itself totally to the immeasurable power of God* coming through the vessel of the Immaculate Heart. She is one of God's secrets, one that we can never fully comprehend: measureless love and grace reach down to us by means of the littlest one, Mary. The lowliest, the poorest, are always the chosen. The most humble and unpretentious are the ones most likely to be singled out by the Lord to be channels of His might. Consecration to the Immaculate Heart lives in this kind of faith. It believes that God can do His most powerful works through someone as simple and weak as Mary, the Virgin of Nazareth. She is not God, but one of us, sharing our human estate and helplessness. Nonetheless, she is filled with God's strength like the stone water-jars at Cana, overflowing by God's power with rich wine for the wedding. She pours out this wine of grace for others. She gives it to us to drink through her love and prayer. She shares in the mediation of Christ. This should cause us no embarrassment. We members of His Body mediate the same grace of Christ as we baptize, forgive, intercede, love. But in her there does not exist the impediment to sharing God's grace which belongs to us because of our sinfulness. In her case, because she is Immaculate (sinless), the Spirit of Jesus rushes upon us through her Heart with such exuberant fullness that there is nothing beyond the ambit of her influence. Consecration acknowledges her universal reign with Christ and welcomes it. The person consecrated to the Immaculate Heart has submitted willingly to God's plan to act through Mary, and revels in the joy of having made that decision. Consecration is an act of humility, by which we bend low as Jesus did when He washed His disciples' feet. In the littleness it admits of itself, it opens the human heart to miracles of transformation. It hastens the reformation of hearts the world over. It quickens The Triumph and the Era of Peace. It averts The Punishment by availing itself of God's mercy, coming through the Mother of Mercy. It shortens the time of The Tribulation, even turning it aside. Consecration assures us of salvation and empowers us to intercede more earnestly and effectively for the salvation of sinners. It is a most necessary ingredient of Our Lady's peace-plan, and will hurry on its fulfillment.

# Chapter Nine

# The Era of Peace

**"I**f people do as I ask, there will be peace."
These words of hope spoken by Our Lady
of Fatima preceded a long litany of the misfortunes
that she predicted would come upon the world if her
requests were not taken seriously. It is imperative to
realize that her assertion still holds: there definitely
will be peace, if people do as she asks. If, even now,
during the "last warnings," we respond with repentance, letting our hearts be cleansed of sin by God's
forgiving grace, there will indeed be peace: peace
first in each person's heart, then throughout the
whole world in society, initiating an Era of Peace,
which she prophesied would inevitably arrive.

Had we listened at the beginning, or at any time
over the years she was remonstrating with us, we
could have averted "wars, famine, persecution of the
Church and of the Holy Father." Many good people
would have been spared martyrdom, hunger would
not have ravaged nations, Russia would have already
been converted, and never would she have been able
to "spread her errors throughout the world," The

Second World War would never have happened.

But these afflictions did take place. Has peace been lost forever? Will the human race obliterate itself with global nuclear war? Is peace a dream, an illusion?

"In the end, My Immaculate Heart will triumph . . . and an Era of Peace will be given to the world." This promise is unconditional. Peace is coming. It will be the peace that Jesus gives, not that which is given by "the world." People will finally do as she asks, and there will be peace. Peace, an era of peace, is surely on its way. It is not an illusion to believe this. The Mother of God has predicted it. Despite human considerations and doubts, failures and sins, wars or punishment, her prophecy will come true "in the end."

*The Era of Peace awaits The Triumph.* Measuring the time that remains before peace arrives is not possible, since the coming of peace depends on The Triumph happening in us beforehand. We must first hold in our hearts the sinlessness of the Immaculate Heart before peace can come. Repentance must route sin before any peace can be ours. Love must override every other consideration, reconciling us all in gentleness, before we can see peace come. Families and neighborhoods, towns and cities, countries and nations must be reconciled before there can be peace. Above all, Christians must be brought together again in one Body which is the Church, before peace can descend on us from heaven. And the peace must be from heaven. Our Lady referred to this by assuring us that peace will "be given" to the world. It will come from God.

Thus the Era of Peace must wait until The Triumph is complete. Already it has begun in those who have heard the message of Our Lady and have changed their lives, striving daily to become holy and pleasing to God, seeking to imitate the Immaculate Heart of Mary with their own hearts. The Warning has already torn untold millions from their sins; in them especially, The Triumph is gaining a foothold. The Miracle will confirm their decision for them and convert many more to follow Jesus. The grace of repentance flowing from these events may well so advance The Triumph that The Punishment will never happen. But the Era of Peace will not arrive until the Triumph of the Immaculate Heart is so complete that the hearts of all of us will have already been converted to peace.

Peace is a gift for the heart, and if a heart is at peace, it can give away peace. Peace in me can make the world around me a more peaceful place for others. By my peace, I am ready to be in friendly relationship with everyone I meet. Peaceful nations are made up of peaceful persons who have chosen peace as a way of life for themselves. There can be no war between nations full of peaceful men and women. A heart transformed by one's own inner peace can give to the world the peace that the world cannot give itself. It is those who share, through repentance and conversion, the peace of Jesus, who will inaugurate the Era of Peace promised to us all.

For these reasons, we must wait, we know not how long, for the Era of Peace. It can be hastened by people of peace, delayed by people who reject peace and embrace sin. We only know that it will certainly come, this mysterious "peace." The Immaculate Heart has promised it.

The Era of Peace *can arrive very soon.* We can hope for a short interval between The Miracle and The Era of Peace, and that The Punishment will not intervene. Should the world be rapidly converted by the marvelous events we have begun to experience in The Warning, it is possible for the Era of Peace to come quickly. After all, "nothing is impossible with God." Perhaps the great wave of intercessory prayer that will well up in the faithful for the conversion of the world will be so effective that The Era of Peace will come without delay. But we have to admit that a longer, even a much longer interval is also possible, and perhaps more likely (given our record of poor response to the messages), and that it may take many hard years before The Triumph is complete and The Era of Peace begins. We simply have no knowledge of how long it will be, after The Miracle, for The Era of Peace to be given to us. Peace may in fact appear only after The Punishment, which God surely will not be eager to see us suffer. We can hope The Era of Peace will come soon, so that through repentance, no punishment will be necessary to bring peace. May the peace of the Lord be with us all by the intercession of Mary, Mother of God. "Holy Mary, Mother of God, pray for us sinners now," in our times, that we may know world-wide peace again, in the Heart of Jesus and your Immaculate Heart.

# THE
# NEW
# TIMES

# Chapter Ten

# "All Will Love Our Hearts"

*T**he whole world will be converted.* To the mind that does not literally believe that "nothing is impossible with God", the previous sentence would seem utterly absurd. Yet, this is what Our Lord assured Conchita would happen when she asked Him the purpose of The Miracle at Garabandal. It would be, He revealed to her, not only for the conversion of Russia that The Miracle would be worked by the Lord, but for the conversion of *the whole world.* Then, to indicate that this conversion would actually be brought about by The Miracle, He stated further, "Thus, all will love Our Hearts." Jesus told Conchita that by The Great Miracle at Garabandal the entire world — "todos" (everybody) — will be converted. Evangelization, the task Jesus handed over to the Church when He ascended, will at last be universally accomplished. The whole world will become The Church.

*World-conversion has happened before in history.* Twice before, a " whole world" (as its inhabitants thought it to be) has been converted. The

Mediterranean world in the early centuries of the Church's mission was completely turned around by the preaching of the Gospel. Another world, the New World of Central and South America, was evangelized with extreme rapidity when Our Lady "of Guadalupe" appeared to Juan Diego, a humble Indian newly converted. His testimony about his encounter with the Mother of God, together with the miraculous image she imprinted of herself on his cloak, led all God's people in that pagan country into the Church. The conversion of Mexico took only seven years thereafter, as eight million were converted. The whole of South America followed the same course, so that today almost half the baptized Catholics in the world live in that "New World."

*A third World-Evangelization is about to break in on us.* But this time it will not be just a segment of the globe's population, thinking of itself as a separate world, that will turn to Him and be saved. Every nation and each person on earth has been opened to the Gospel by The Warning. The Miracle will draw them toward the Church. These apocalyptic events will make it unquestionable that Jesus is truly Lord and that we must enter into Him and His Church to be saved.

*The Church is being prepared.* The Lord has been readying His Church for the greatest of its missionary efforts, the evangelization of the modern world. Vatican Council II irrevocably altered the direction of the Catholic Church, summoning us back to our primitive fervor and biblical roots, charting for us a new course which has for its destination the conversion of the entire world. The Council Fathers speak not only to the Church itself gathered around the successor of Saint Peter, the Pope, but to our "separated brethren" of the other Christian Churches, and also to the world that is neither Catholic nor Christian. The bishops break the barriers to dialogue by addressing in the Council even those who have never heard the Word of Christ. Their attitude restimulates in us the belief that God's Word still has all the power and life it needs to redeem the masses of humanity. The Bishops of the Council assumed the responsibility, issuing from Christ's command, to preach the Gospel to all the nations on the face of the earth. For centuries there have been insuperable obstacles, political, economic, cultural, and otherwise, to this enterprise. But today, many of the forces once antithetical to evangelizing are crumbling. Because of modern technological advances, improvements in communications, political cooperation among many nations, multi-national resources, and other developments, we are fast moving toward geopolitical unity. A similar unity was characteristic of the Roman world in the time of Christ and the apostolic Church. For some three hundred years the Mediterranean Sea was considered a "Roman Lake" across which missionaries like Saint Paul had free access to all the civilized world they knew, and to all its population centers. The "Pax Romana," or Roman Peace, reigned under the Caesars. Not without difficulty, but blessed by the world-situation, the people of the Roman Empire, slave and free, rich or poor, commoner, nobleman, emperor, eventually all entered the Church through the preaching of the apostles of the time. God had made ready the world, in the fullness of time, for the mystery and power of the "Good News" of Jesus Christ. With the indomitable strength and guidance of the Holy

Spirit, the spread of the Gospel and the Church met with total success.

Today the Catholic Church looks toward her future with a new awareness of her call to evangelize. Not only did a recent Synod of Bishops (1974) state their commitment to it, but from the grassroots, among Catholics particularly, a new zeal to proclaim the Gospel throughout the whole world is becoming evident. God is preparing His Church for the great age of evangelization that is about to appear.

*The whole world will be evangelized.* The Marian apparitions, especially those at Fatima and Garabandal, invite the human race to repentance and salvation. Our Lady of Fatima declared that an Era of Peace would be "given to the world." At Garabandal, Our Lord promised "the conversion of the *whole world.*" The Era of Peace, The Triumph of the Immaculate Heart, and the Conversion of the Whole World were all predicted as an unconditional and definite future. All three imply the evangelization of the globe. An Age of Evangelization will begin soon, and to us who are His Church, He still commands, "Go into the whole world and preach the Gospel to every creature" (Mark 16:15). We must prepare ourselves for this, the greatest of God's works in history. The Father is going to send us, his little ones, to the four corners of the earth to bring the good news to everyone.

*The Warning prepares the Church.* It is the most compelling preparation the Lord could have given us for the coming Age of Evangelization. By The Warning, God demands that we face our sinfulness, always the major obstacle to the spread of the Gospel, and repent. We must be purified. The Warning also reveals to us that our times are unique, unlike any other times, and that a new age is dawning for which we must be ready. There have been "wars and rumors of wars," and we have been tempted to panic, as if the end were at hand. But Jesus tells us, "that is not yet the end" (Matthew 24:6). "This good news of the kingdom will be proclaimed to all the nations. Only after that will the end come"(Matthew 24:16). Could it be that he was referring to the Age of Evangelization we have been describing? To a priest with whom she was discussing the prophecies of Garabandal, Conchita stated, "When you see The Warning, you will know that we have opened up the end of time." This assertion is offered as her own opinion; she is not directly quoting Our Lady. But on other occasions she has insisted that we are near "the end of *the times*." The least we may infer from these declarations is that if they are accurate in their assessment of our moment of history, a great and final epoch is about to begin: The Era of Peace and the Age of Evangelization. The Warning is the "sign of the times" which announces to us the "New Times" the period of history when God will act in greater power than ever before to bring the Gospel, through His Church, to every creature. All will come to love the Hearts of Jesus and Mary, and love will reign in the world. The Warning was the first of these acts of power. It is preparing us all for the age of glory that is approaching.

*The Church will be reunited.* Time and again the Bishops attending the Synod on Evangelization in 1974 voiced their conviction in speeches to that august body that unless the Church again becomes one, it is futile to expect the evangelization of the world to develop. Our disunity is an evident scandal and a contradiction to the demands of the Gospel. The Holy Catholic Church must become one again in order to be recognizable to the nations as the Church that Jesus established. Unity is its distinguishing characteristic. But our common sinfulness has led us astray; history records break after break in the threads that weave together the seamless robe of Christ. Unity, true and full unity, must be attained once more before the evangelization of the world can even be considered likely.

Such unity has to be a gift from the Lord. Pope John Paul II has made assertions along this vein a number of times when referring to the divided condition of today's churches. His conviction that unity must come from God as grace and favor was expressed in his invitation to the leaders of the Christian world to journey to Rome for Pentecost Sunday in 1981 (June 7th) to first pray together to the Holy Spirit for unity, rather than immediately "discuss our differences" (his words).

*God is determined to reunite His Church.*The most excruciating pain the members of all the Christian churches felt on the day of The Warning was to see the harm we have all done to one another by not remaining one in heart and mind. By now the whole world would have become Christian, and many saved from perdition in centuries gone by, if we had continued to be faithful to one another. The Warning has made us aware of the enormity of this corporate sin of which all of us are to some degree guilty. We require a deep renewal of heart in order to reverse this division, and to embrace the full

Catholic unity to which the Lord now directs us. Not only so-called "non-Catholics," but Catholics too, the Lord presses to lay down their cherished prejudices. Our hardness must be melted away for all hearts to flow together into one compact unity.

*The conversion of Russia* will be the turning point for the reunion of all Christians. It is required by the Lord, according to the Fatima messages, that the Consecration of that country to the Immaculate Heart be enacted by the Pope *in union with all the Bishops of the world.* The promise that Russia will be converted by this action will leave no doubt, after conversion follows swiftly, that it happened 1) by the intercession of the Immaculate Heart, and 2) by the authority of the Pope and the Bishops; it will establish before all eyes the traditional teaching of the Catholic Church concerning the Pope and Mary. It will be disconcerting to many that the Pope, the authority of the Church to bind and to loose (through him and the other Bishops), and Mary's power as channel of intercession and grace will be shown to be not the problem impeding Christian unity, but rather the solution to the problem. God will set our presuppositions on their heads. Unity will come because God wills it, because He has set out the way it shall be achieved, and because He, not we, is the giver of Unity.

*The new Church will be humble.* We will come together again in mutual forgiveness. Whatever gifts of the Spirit a particular church has received or rediscovered, it will share gladly with the others. The whole Church will be enriched by us all being together again in one Body. A fully empowered Church will become, in each member, evangelizer, apostle, preacher, servant. There will not only be chosen apostles who will go out into the highways and byways to compel them to come in; everyone will realize and carry out the mission given to us all: " Preach the Gospel everywhere! " It will be an age of conversion unlike any other. The entire Church, gathered together again by its own conversion into unity, will turn outward to bring in the harvest, lying in wait, ripe for reaping.

*The Church reunited will be the Sign of Evangelization.* Even though The Warning, The Miracle, and The Punishment (if it comes) will be signs for the whole world, they are given to focus our attention on the Great Sign of the Church itself, reunited by the Spirit, from which salvation must come. It is because we have stifled her witness by our sins that The Warning and The Miracle have become necessary. Prodigies and wonders alert us to where the mystery of the Church can be discovered. To point us toward the Church, God has determined that The Miracle will coincide with an important ecclesiastical event. The Miracle will take place on a Thursday evening at 8:30, to remind us that we find unity at the supper-table of the Church, for the Holy Eucharist was founded on that day and time of evening. The Miracle will happen on the Feast-day of a Martyr of the Church, again emphasizing that it was in unity with the Church that this martyr-saint gave his or her life in such love. The visible head of the Church, the Pope, and the Bishops, heads of the Church in their dioceses and eparchies, are, personally, sacramental signs of the unity of the Church who are called by their ministry to protect our oneness. The Miracle is to bring about the conversion of Russia and of the whole world; it will somehow be linked with the collegial consecration of Russia to the Immaculate Heart. The connection of this action of the Catholic Bishops united with the Pope will convince those of us who doubt it that God's power is with the Church united to that body, and this again will lead us toward a true Catholic unity with them. God wants us to again accept the Church as a credible witness to His truth, and to this end He will work these wonders to persuade us to seek Him with, through, and in His One True Church. It is His way of redeeming us, the "incarnational" way, whereby He gives us to one another so that we will find Him with, through, and in one another. We must allow ourselves to be taken into that Church and led by it. His Body is the Church, with all the gifts of the Holy Spirit as her patrimony, not excluding the Pope, Church authority and teaching, the Bishops and Priests, Mary, the Holy Eucharist and the other Sacraments, including Confession and indissoluble Matrimony. Reunited in the fullness of her gifts, the Church will shine like the sun before the nations. They will see that she alone offers and can give salvation, and they will stream into that heavenly city from all the corners of the earth.

*The Church lives in time*, and it will take time for the conversion of the world to take place and for evangelization to be completed. God can pierce time as He did during The Warning, but the spread of the message depends ordinarily, even after such a prodigy as The Warning, on the ministry of the Church *in time*. There has to be, therefore, an Era of Peace, to allow evangelization to unfold. The world will not be brought into the Church overnight, nor without struggle, persecution, hardship and pain. Not everyone has been so renovated by The Warning that all will immediately embrace the Christian faith. Local churches will need opportunity to become fully united and mature, strong enough to engage in the work of evangelizing. The process that began in Jerusalem and Antioch over nineteen centuries ago will have to be repeated, this time on a world-wide basis. A well-developed system of instruction, catechesis, pastoral care and mutual support must first blossom, to render recognizable the Church where all can find salvation. The Church must be properly organized to evangelize the world, and the world may be hesitant to surrender at once to the demands of living the full implications of the mystery of Church. The complete conversion of the world by the Church newly reunited will require much time. We will need the Era of Peace.

*What will the Church of the Era of Peace be like?* The prophecy given at Garabandal creating the greatest curiosity concerns the present Pope. Conchita tells us Our Lady revealed that "There will be only two more Popes after Paul VI, but that does not mean the end of the world." This difficult prediction implies that during the last years of history remaining before the Second Coming of Christ, the Church will have no Pope. Will it also be the Era of Peace? Or will the Era of Peace be so short that this present Pope, John Paul II, who according to the prophecy is the last one, will live to the end of it, when persecution begins again and only a short time is left before the world ends? Or can it signify that a form of Church unity will be embraced where the Petrine office will be exercised by more than one person or by a college of Patriarchs, somewhat after the manner of the Orthodox Church? The meaning of Mary's words is obscure, but she does link this prophecy about the last Pope with the "end of *the times*."

Perhaps the purpose the Blessed Virgin has in unveiling this unusual prediction is to prepare us for unprecedented organizational shifts in the structure of the Church of the future. Reunion and world-evangelization will require enormous alteration of attitudes and methods to accomplish the tasks at hand. The Church, it appears, will be vastly different from the one we are used to now, and light-years away from the Church as it was before the Second Vatican Council.

## Conclusion

This book has been written to prepare minds for the events to come. For over twenty years, the revelations of Garabandal have been held in doubt and confusion, through circumstances beyond the control of any of us. This situation was in the plan of God, and was predicted by Our Lady herself at Garabandal. But now The Warning has confirmed all those events, and dispelled the fog hanging over the apparitions that occurred there. Her words and lessons in that little mountain village also reaffirm and authenticate the Marian apparitions of the past, and link them all in a remarkable tapestry of prophecy that singles out the years we are passing through as the most important in history. She has given us the "Last Warnings," and we know we are seeing the "End of the Times." We are on the threshold of a new age, an Era of Peace, a time of evangelization without comparison. God is doing everything to prepare us. This book has attempted to bring to center-focus the elements of the basic message the Mother of God has been bringing to the world for over one hundred and fifty years.

God Himself has begun, by The Warning, to dramatically make clear to us that what Mary has proclaimed has been true all along. We can all see for ourselves what God is doing, because He is making His works apparent. No one can sincerely maintain, from now on, that there is no God or that He has no power. We are experiencing His judgement upon our world, which has drifted so far from Him. In His mercy, He now gives us the opportunity to turn back to Him before it is too late.

*We must wait now for The Miracle,* which will surely ensue within a year of the date of The Warning. It will eventually convert the whole world. A new world is being born. There are wars and rumors of wars, but we are not to panic, for "the end is not yet." There is an Era of Peace stretching out before us. We must reach out for it, grasp it, and give it to one another. We cannot delay any longer. The time is now.